WHY WE *Really* L🐾VE DOGS

WHY WE Really LOVE DOGS

A Bark & Smile™ Book

KIM LEVIN

Andrews McMeel
Publishing

Kansas City

00 01 02 03 04 TWP 10 9 8 7 6 5 4 3 2 1

ISBN: 0-7407-0670-5

Library of Congress Catalog Card Number: 99-68291

Book design by Lisa Martin

www.barkandsmile.com

───── ATTENTION: SCHOOLS AND BUSINESSES ─────

Andrews McMeel books are available at quantity discounts with bulk purchase for educational, business, or sales promotional use. For information, please write to: Special Sales Department, Andrews McMeel Publishing, 4520 Main Street, Kansas City, Missouri 64111.

For John and Charlie

Acknowledgments

After my first book, *Why We Love Dogs*, was published in 1998, I received many phone calls and E-mails from people who had seen the book and wanted their dogs captured on film. Many of those dogs appear on these pages.

I wish to extend my gratitude to all of the owners whose dogs appear in *Why We Really Love Dogs*. To all of the incredible dogs who appear in *Why We Really Love Dogs* . . . I had such a great time photographing you. Thank you for making what I do so much fun and meaningful.

Thank you to Dorothy O'Brien and everyone else at Andrews McMeel Publishing who shares my love of dogs and their significance to our lives.

Special thanks to Rick for spending so much time helping me with all of my Bark & Smile™ endeavors. And of course, thank you to John for more than I can write on one page.

WHY WE Really LOVE DOGS

"Do I know you?"

because they like to swing

because they carry our bags

because they sit for cookies

because they grin

because they reminisce

because they question

because they look like twins

because they tilt to the left . . .

. . . and to the right

because they pose for the camera

"Say what?"

because they hang out in the woods

because they compete for cuteness

because they're expressive

because they love treats . . .

. . . but pay the price

because they have big heads

because they ride in wagons

because they roll over . . .

. . . and over

. . . and over

. . . and over

"Hike!"

because their heads are in the clouds

because they wear socks

because they're clumsy

"My . . . what big teeth you have!"

because they play peekaboo

because they're in-your-face

because they pant

because they eat shoes

because they're original

"Hello."

because they clash

because they pound the pavement

because they're sweet

because they can touch their
noses with their tongues

because they beg

"I'm the king of the world!"

because they get embarrassed

because they jump for joy

because they hide

because they make
themselves comfortable

because they blend right in

because they give us "the look"

"Hey, blue eyes."

because they stare us down

because they come in big and small sizes

because they're macho

because they hang out on the porch

"I'm in heaven."

because they ponder

because they lie in the leaves

because they play piggyback . . .

. . . and horseyback

because they have great eyes

because they go for afternoon strolls

because you can tell when they're lying

because they're lanky

because they smile while they stretch

"Wanna play?"

because they love each other

because they get their hair done

because they fetch

because they oink

because they love a good nap

because they run wild and free

because they wear sweaters . . .

. . . and jackets

"Welcome home!"

because they stick their tongues out at us

because they laugh . . .

. . . and sing

. . . and they just plain look funny